# The Devil Takes the Highway

## The Legend of Swift Nick Navison

Marie Campbell

Copyright © 2011 - Marie Campbell.

All rights reserved. No part of this publication may be reproduced in any form or by any means - graphic, electronic, mechanical, including photocopying, recording, taping or information storage and retrieval systems - without the prior permission in writing of the publishers.

ISBN 978-0-9528174-3-7

Published by:
wwpublishing
Midway Cottage
Eastgate
Hornsea
East Yorkshire
HU18 1DP
Contact  www@wwbooks.net

## Part One

| | |
|---|---|
| The Life of Nevison | 1 |
| Early Days | 3 |
| London Beckons | 4 |
| Up and Away! Holland and Dunkirk | 6 |
| Extortion Racket Newark | 7 |
| On the Road Give and Take | 7 |
| 1661 Wealthy Grazier Robbed Home-Ward-Bound | 9 |
| Bold Nevison Helps Farmer | 11 |
| Nevison Robs Near London | 12 |
| 'As Common as Crows' | 13 |
| 1668 Escape from York Castle | 14 |
| 1674 Wakefield Prison | 14 |
| 1676 Things go Wrong then Right | 16 |
| 1676 George Skipwith Informer | 17 |
| 1676 Nevison Arrested | 18 |
| 1676 The Ride Kent to York | 18 |
| 1606 John Lepstone London to York | 22 |
| Mr Powell, The Great Walker | 22 |
| Who Was Harris? | 22 |
| What Odds? | 23 |
| Coach Travel | 23 |
| Rookwood | 24 |
| Nevison's One-Eyed Mare | 24 |
| Nevison Horse Whisperer | 25 |
| False Hearted Love | 26 |
| The Highwayman (in part) | 26 |
| Turn Coat | 27 |
| Penal Transportation | 28 |
| 1681 Breaks Loose | 29 |
| Leicester Jail-Plague-Daring Escape | 30 |
| Moon Men | 32 |
| Nevison Refuses to Rob Old Woman | 34 |

## Part Two: THE BIRD IS IN THE CAGE

| | |
|---|---|
| Dark and Deadly Deed at Howley | 36 |
| Fletcher Gravemarker | 37 |
| Here Nevison Killed Fletcher | 38 |
| Look Upon a Traitor - The Net Tightens | 38 |
| Beware The Ides of March | 42 |
| Mournful Words of a Bellman | 43 |
| Death Come, Quickly Away! | 46 |
| Mystery of Inn and Nevison's Chattels | 48 |
| Rev. Heywood's Thoughts on Nevison | 50 |
| Burial | 51 |
| York Castle Prison | 52 |
| The Wortley's of Wortley Hall | 54 |
| Nevison's Real Father | 56 |
| St. Helen Wells in the Parish of Roystone | 57 |

## Part Three: NEVISON'S BOLT HOLES'

| | |
|---|---|
| Ackworth Old Hall | 60 |
| Nevison House | 61 |
| Ardsley Old Hall | 62 |
| Parcevall Hall, near Skipton | 62 |
| Swainby | 66 |
| At the Sign of the Black Horse | 66 |
| Wentbridge and Brockdale | 66 |
| Captain Nevison a Craven Legend | 68 |
| The Ebbing and Flowing Well, Giggleswick | 75 |
| Polyolbion (in part) | 77 |
| Church of St. Alkelda, Giggleswick | 78 |
| Pontefract's Nevison Leap | 81 |
| A Name to Conjure With | 82 |
| Nevison Coat of Arms | 83 |

## PART ONE

## THE LIFE OF NEVISON

The old parish register states that Johannes, Filius (John, father of) a second son, John Nevison was baptised at Tankersley, Yorkshire on 10th September 1648. John had an elder brother named William some nine years older than he, born in Pontefract sometime in January 1639. Now, as then, mystery still surrounds which brother was actually the highwayman, later dubbed 'Swift Nicks' by King Charles II. Only the Nevison family and those closest to them would have known his true identity. For the purpose of this book, and to avoid confusion, I shall refer to him only as Nevison unless otherwise stated in quotes.

John Nevison is recorded has having died in York on 15th March 1684 the very day 'Swift Nick' met his death on the gallows in the same place, however, it seems more likely, that it was actually the elder brother, William, who was tried, convicted and condemned as a highwayman in his brother's name. This is because John, would have been far too young at the time he was supposed to have run away and afterwards joined the army.

We shall probably never really know the true identity of this particular infamous High Toby, for dates and times differ widely in the many accounts of his life which have tumbled down through the centuries.

It was well documented that Nevison was not averse to using other alias's sometimes too, which also adds to the confusion surrounding his life and times. But, whatever his forename, it cannot detract from the fact that the man

Nevison, even in his own time, was a great legend.
To complicate matters further dates of this time vary, because there was two calendars' in operation at the same time. The old Julian calendar began the year on 25$^{th}$ March whilst the new Gregorian calendar began the year just as we do today on the 1$^{st}$ January. Also, because even official accounts were not altogether accurate either, it is very difficult to establish an exact date in time of Nevison's exploits. Even York Castle records erroneously quote Nevison's family name as being Brace or Bracey (probably through false information) and that he hailed from Burton Agnes, Yorkshire, where he had an uncle. It is this account which also says that Nevison was a married man and that his wife lived beyond the town of Pontefract (a fact later substantiated by John Hobson in his diary dated March 10$^{th}$ 1732. In it he writes; "Coz. (Cousin) Beet, at our house, sayd the wife of Nevison, the hywayman, died at Kirby aged 109 years." Looking at parish registers the Beet family married into the Hobson family, and this may have been the reason for cousin Beet living at the house of John Hobson. It appears then, that 'Cousin Beet' was not a blood relative of Mr Hobson's.

If Cousin Beet had wed one of the brothers which one was she married too? If it were William, that would make him about 16 years younger than her, whereas John Nevison would be 25 years her junior. Although not impossible – it is improbable, especially as we are told they had a daughter together who died aged 8 on September 11$^{th}$ 1710 – this would make cousin Beet about 79 years old when she gave birth, unless of course, the date of birth of the child was much earlier.

John Nevison, the father of the two boys in question, was a native of Pontefract, born about 1619. He found a wife having married her in 1638 at the age of twenty. Unfortunately, I do not have a name for Mrs Nevison. The family lived at Wortley, close to the towns of both Sheffield, and Barnsley, South Yorkshire, where Mr John Nevison senior apparently earned an honest living, working as a servant, in the service of the Earl of Wharncliffe, Sir Francis Wortley, whose ancestral seat was Wortley Hall. The Nevison family may have lived at Tividale Cottage circa 1600, in the small village of Wortley. The cottage being rebuilt in 1983. This building was supposed to have been the home of Headmaster and Chapelwarden, William Nevison (or John?) who passed away in 1723. Mr J. A. Barstow thought this may also have been the place where Nevison, the highwayman was born. Of both boys upbringing, non-conformist preacher Oliver Heywood was later to write that, Mistress Cotton told him she lived near the Nevison family and knew them very well. She does not mention the mother, but claims the brothers had been "brought up prophanely..."

## EARLY DAYS

Nevison was an intelligent boy, who received a decent education. However, as a teenager he fell in with a group of youths, about his own age, and got into no end of mischief. He seems to have ever had his eye on the main chance, and, so it was, when barely fourteen or fifteen, he stole poultry and fruit from a nearby orchard together with a silver spoon, worth about £10 from his own father

At school the following day the master flogged him for the crime. "The punishment was the subject of a night's meditation, which issued into a resolution of revenge on his schoolmaster, whatever fate he met with in the execution thereof; to which end having hit on a project for his purpose, and lying in his father's chamber, he got up softly before such time as the day appeared, and hearing that his father slept, he put his hand into his pocket, where he found a key of his closet, (safe) which, unperceived, he drew thence, and down he creeps, where he supplies himself with what cash he could readily find, which amounted to about £10, and knowing that his school master owned a horse he took a particular delight knowing that it grazed behind his house, he got a bridle and saddle from his father's stable, and an hour before morning, mounted, and arrived at London within four days..." And so it was that young Nevison, drawn as a moth to a flame, began his new career on the open road – a life full of adventure, danger and daring do.

## LONDON BECKONS

It took the boy four days to negotiate his way to the great Metropolis, which for one so young, was a great feat, since no signposts or maps existed at that time to guide the weary wayfarer on his way. Approaching the outskirts of the city by evening, Nevison, fearful of being recognised slit the unfortunate pony's throat, afterwards changing into clean clothing he had brought with him. Having reached the capital city on foot, and giving a false name (possibly Johnson) he managed to secure a job working as a brewer's lad.

He was to remain in this post for two or three years, until his darker side got the better of him when he could not resist taking advantage of his master's counting clerk who had fallen into a drunken stupor one evening after drinking the master's liquor. Nimbly, Nevison removed the keys to the strong box from the drunken man's person, and upon rifling the safe he emptied out the contents and made off with his ill-gotten gains after donning a disguise. The luckless brewer together with emissaries of the law sought after him for many days, but the fugitive had gotten clean away from London.

A London street on a rainy day in the days of Queen Elizabeth

## UP AND AWAY! HOLLAND AND DUNKIRK

With the stolen £200 burning a hole in his pocket, the young thief sailed to Holland. Here he fell in with a burger master's daughter. He persuaded the girl to steal a large amount of cash and jewellery belonging to her father. What became of the girl afterwards remains a mystery, but young Nevison was handed a custodial sentence for his part in the heist.

Wiping the prison stench from his person after a daring escape, Nevison enlisted in 1658 (if this date is correct then it proves that John Nevison would have been but ten years old at the time!) as a volunteer under the command of the Duke of York (who later rose to King James II). Nevison, having joined as an English volunteer, took part in the raise of the Siege of Dunkirk the same year. His time in battle was well spent. Although a brave youth at heart, he felt that he was not suited to military life. With money honestly earned, he deserted the army, and set course with all speed, back to his native soil. As stage coaches were now travelling to York (since 1658) a plan formed in his mind as to how he could make easy money.

Once in England, he equipped himself for a life on the open road, being an adroit horseman, he chose an animal he thought best suited to his particular needs. He also purchased a sword, and a good set of pistols. And so it was that in 1660 Nevison, the Highwayman was born...

## EXTORTION RACKET NEWARK

High-spirited Nevison, found himself drawn to the Old North Road where there was plenty easy pickings to be had. At that time he chiefly worked without an accomplice. The 'prentice discovered a liking to his new vocation, and took money from almost everyone who passed him by. He did not look at this as robbery for he preferred to call it 'borrowing'. Should he have call to rob a poor person, he often returned the money by way of 'borrowing' from a wealthy body!

Newark being on the Old North Road became just one of the many hubs of Nevison's nest of thieves and other freebooters. His territory generally ran from Huntingdon in the south to York in the north. An extortion racket was set up by him. His gang extracted money from innkeepers and businessmen alike. Nevison termed it his; 'quarterly contributions'. This must have been one of the earliest informal 'insurance policies' in the land. If his victims paid, he and his cohorts shielded them from other thieves and highwaymen! If not then they must take their chances... Life at that time must have felt good in a highwayman-kind-of-way that was until the luck ran out, and, he found himself back in prison for a spell, which happened quite a lot.

## ON THE ROAD — GIVE AND TAKE

One day Nevison, using the alias of Johnson, met two countrymen on the road, who told him that they had already been robbed of £40 by three highwaymen and warned him to go careful for there was danger ahead.

Put out by this revelation, he bid the farmers "turn back with me, and show me the way they took, and my life to a farthing, I'll make them return your money..." True to his word, upon approaching one of the three rogues, Nevison said, "Sir, by your garb and colour of your horse, you should be one of those I am looking after; and if so, my business is to tell you that you borrowed of two friends of mine £40, which they desired of me to demand of you, and, which before we part, you must restore." The thief denied having stolen the money, and, looking round at his audience, he declared, "Damn me, Sir! Is the fellow mad? "So mad," Nevison retorted, "As that your life shall answer to me if you do not give me better satisfaction."

At this Nevison grabbed his opponent, with one hand, thus preventing him from drawing either sword or pistol, whilst at the same time, securing the reins of his horse. Seeing no way out, "Jack" (a 17th century term meaning highwayman) begged for his scrawny life to be spared. "No (says Nevison) 'tis not that I seek for, but the money you robbed these two men of, who riding up to me, which you must refund." The thief was forced to yield.

Nevison proceeded to take the "Jacks" horse from him, and, after leaving the luckless robber in the hands of the two country victims, he rode out on the thief's horse in search of the other two highwaymen. On reaching a common he soon drew close to the remaining thieves, who had mistaken him for their partner-in-crime calling over "How now Jack, (says one of them) what made you engage with yon fellow?"
"No gentlemen," replies Nevison, "you are mistaken in your man Thomas, by the token of his horse and arms, he

hath sent me to you by reason of his life, which comes to no less than the prize of the day, and if you presently surrender, you may go about your business; if not I must have a little dispute with you at sword and pistol." One of them let fly at him; but missing his aim, received Nevison's bullet into his right shoulder; and being thereby disabled. Nevison about to discharge at the other robber called for them to return the money to him and all the other cash they might have upon them, which amounted to £150 and some silver coinage.

True to his word our hero of the day released the third robber and handed the £40 back to the country gentlemen with a caution for the future, "to look better after it, and not like cowards as they were, to surrender the same on any such terms again." Nevison then pocketed the remaining £110 for himself!

### 1661 WEALTHY GRAZIER ROBBED —

### HOMEWARD BOUND

A wealthy country grazier who had just received a hefty payment for the sale of his cattle was to provide Nevison with a further £450 in the year of 1661. Following this haul and having a bounty placed upon his head on 31st October (as published in The London Gazette) of that year by the Governor of York prison he decided that the risks of his job had become too great, and he, tired of living on the road decided that it would be more prudent to retire, keep his head down, and lead an honest life, well at least for a time...

**Thus it was that the now wealthy, prodigal son, returned to his Yorkshire home and into his joyous father's open arms, (who had no way of knowing what had become of his erring son and must have believed him dead after an absence of several years.) Undetected by the law, Nevison, now a wealthy young man, settled down, becoming a model son to his father John, who was but aged 42 years old at that time.**

Father and Son Lavater

All went well until the death of his father, and it was not long before the "model son" took to the open road once more in order to earn his living.

## BOLD NEVISON HELPS FARMER

In the early days Nevison, took to hijacking travellers in the Hope Valley. Having an eye on the main chance he was always more than ready to help the poor. One day he met a farmer who had just sold his cattle at Bakewell market. Falling into conversation whilst the pair travelled toward Stoke, but on having reached the edge of a wood Nevison turned his pistol toward the man, taking his gold coins from him. The farmer pleaded with the highwayman saying if he stole the money, his family would be made homeless. Adding, that he had been forced to sell his animals, in order to raise the due rent, which had to be paid by Michaelmas. Afterwards the poor man knew not what to do for he was now rent-less, thanks to Nevison. Unable to sleep on Michaelmas Eve he heard two distinct shots fired around midnight from the direction of Grindleford Bridge. Soon after he heard the sound of beating hoofs heading towards his front door. There was the sound of breaking glass and horses hoofs retreating away into the distance before the farmer dared investigate. To his utter amazement he found a bag on the floor which had been thrown through the broken window filled with more gold than he needed!

This second tale concerning the same story changes in the telling; from the pages of Criminal Chronicles of York Castle by William Kaye 1867, repeated by Charles G. Harper 1901; "On one occasion, at a small village public-house, where he (Nevison) was staying, hearing the conversation about a small farmer with a large family being sold up, and finding the bailiff to be one of the company, with the cash (the proceeds of the sale) upon him, he resolved to rob him of it. He called for a candle, it being evening, and being shown to bed by the landlord, soon arranged his plan. He got out of the window, and had not long to wait before the object of his night's exploit appeared. At a very short distance he presented his pistol, and demanded the man's money in a tone and manner which the poor bailiff well understood. He begged for his life, and very submissively gave up every farthing of the money. Returning to his lodgings by the same way as he came. Nevison passed a good night, congratulating himself on the pleasure he should have in restoring back to the poor farmer and his family the money for which their little all had been sold, which he did the next day, not stopping a single penny. Nevison frequently visited the farmer afterwards on his journeys, and ultimately acquainted him with the whole affair."

## NEVISON ROBS NEAR LONDON

In yet another daring escapade near London, Nevison robbed a man empowered by the Commonwealth to collect fines levied on the Royalists — the latter, being a cause close to the highwayman's heart, being a true Loyalist himself. Having first apologized to the ladies traveling alongside the money collector (usurer), he warned the woman that he must borrow one of the coach horses, but promised to return the animal in good time

Nevison, having already lifted sixty pieces of gold from the collection man, forced him into accompanying him some distance away from the coach and made him make a bill out to the tune of £500 (made out to the bearer, of course,) upon a scrivener in London. A short time afterwards the collection man returned to the coaching inn, where the ladies were waiting, he told them that he had been in fear of his life until Nevison had secured the bill from him. The robber rode all through the night so that he might draw the money before the collector had chance to stop it.
Note; The Bank of England did not begin trading until 1694, previous to this Goldsmiths, in exchange for gold gave out bills to the public.

### "AS COMMON AS CROWS."

It must be said that most highwaymen were not as audacious and as clever as Nevison. This being illustrated so well in this little story as told about 'Lord A' who had declared to all and sundry that no highwayman would ever take his gold. This challenge was soon taken up by a highwayman who stopped his carriage and sticking his pistols through the carriage window demanded money or his life. Saying, "I think my Lord; you've declared that no highwayman could ever rob you?" "True," replied the lord, "nor should I let you rob me now, if it were not for that dark figure behind you." The highwayman turned his head to see behind him. Too late! The lord grabbed the pistol, and shot the robber dead. This would not have happened to Nevison, for he possessed much self-preservation, and was very intuitive. In the early days he often preferred working alone seeking out mail coaches and the like which he viewed as fat purses on wheels! Highwaymen did not always work by the roadside, as Sir John Cutler, a wealthy London merchant found out, when almost being accosted by two highwaymen, who laid in wait for him at his home at

Gawthorpe Hall, Yorkshire (made famous by the Bronte connection). Sir John was so nervous that he took up residence in a cottage situated the nearby village with only his man servant for company "where he lived secure from attack."

## 1668 ESCAPE FROM YORK CASTLE

Nevison having escaped from York Castle, although having been confined in a locked prison cell and, though closely guarded, he still outwitted (or bribed) his jailor and escaped, prior to his being sentenced for his part in a crime! And so it was that in December 1668 a reward was set for £20 for any person who could capture the highwayman which led to an arrest.

On the 18th November 1669 the London Gazette again published a proclamation offering a reward of £20 for the recapture of the highwayman Nevison.

## 1674 WAKEFIELD PRISON

By 1674 it was noted in a pamphlet entitled Bloody News from Yorkshire describes how a running battle took place between fifteen butchers on their way to Northallerton Fair and Nevison's gang of twenty highwaymen who laid in wait for them. Apparently, fight was so fierce that seven of the butchers died at the scene, their names being; Thomas Simpson, Ralph Green, George Waterhouse, Gregory Smith, Will Brand, Edward Hewitt and last but not least Francis Miles.

The robbers made off with almost £1000. During the battle Nevison lost three of his men and later another four of their number were killed by their pursuers. The thirteen thieves remaining were sent to York Castle. Two of the men claimed to have been under the tutorage of the famous French highwayman Claude Du-val and had formally belonged to his gang. Du-val born in 1643 was executed on 21st January 1670. Was Nevison one of these to men? Royalist Claude Du-val is said to haunt The Holt Hotel, (an old coaching inn on the Oxford Road, Oxfordshire.)

Nonconformist, Oliver Heywood complained that; "I have seen him ( Nevison ) pass ordinarily in the road, he led his horse lately down the street at Wakefield, was generally known, yet none were so hardy as to lay hands on him, tho there was £20 by proclamation to him that should take him, but he is last gone, and has left much debt at several ale houses in the country where he haunted." Heywood a religious man believed Nevison to be a wicked servant of the Devil himself, even said that he was a drudge to Satan! Calling him a furious beast that devoured the country and would be better if all his ilk were gotten rid of and their "precious souls tormented to hell to all eternity.... It may be the promotion to the gallows — that all his thievish ways and drinking companions might learn... to leave their wicked ways and fear God!" No doubt Heywood's prayers were answered when Nevison was eventually re-captured near Wakefield in 1674 York Castle Records say that; "He was next captured at Wakefield charged with a string of crimes, of which he was convicted, and sentenced to be hanged, but managed to break out of prison, and again took to the road."

## 1676 THINGS GO WRONG THEN RIGHT

In 1676 a further reward of £20 was offered for the apprehension of the highwayman Nevison, who had lately escaped from York Castle prison. It appears that York Prison was unable to keep safely the person until his or her fate shall be determined by the due course of law.

This was just the beginning of things going wrong for Nevison, for it was also in 1676 that one of his closest associates, Adam Hawksworth, landlord of Ringstone Hill Inn, Brierley, near Wakefield, West Yorkshire, was forced to pay a huge fine. This was imposed upon him by magistrates at the Rotherham Sessions held in 1676, for allowing "lewd fellows who infest the road" to enter his hostelry, (meaning Nevison, and others of the same ilk). Actually, the 1604 Act of Parliament stated that; "The ancient, true and principle use of ale houses, was for the lodging of way-faring people and for the supply of the wants of such as were not able by greater quantities, to make their provisions of victuals, and not for entertaining and harbouring of lewd, and idle people, to spend their money, and their time, in a lewd and drunken manner." Now and then the Government would be forced to issue a proclamation against the harbouring of these knights-of-the-road. It was true to say that Hawksworth's house was known to be of such ill-repute, that he lost not only his money, but also his licence to trade as a landlord! His business was immediately closed down by the Rotherham authorities. Even in Saxon times there were complaints the inns were the focal point for highwaymen and pickpockets. In the time of Nevison and his like, taverns such as Hawksworth's had become natural meeting places and safe houses.

Landlords took backhanders, keeping their mouths shut when the law came sniffing around.

Not far from Adam Hawksworth's inn grew an old English oak tree, its girth measuring a huge twenty-seven feet. Three foot above the ground was a large cavity, and it was here that Nevison is thought to have hidden his ill-gotten booty from prying eyes and nimble fingers of other thieves in the locality. The tree existed in 1890 but I do not know if it still exists today.

## 1676 GEORGE SKIPWITH INFORMER

George Skipwith of Howden, in the West Riding was examined by local magistrates in March 1676. Skipwith confessed that he knew Nevison but believed he went under the alias of John Brace or Bracey he also gave the names of Nevison's accomplices as being; Tankered, John Bracey and Edmund Bracy. Skipwith said Nevison had recently been living with an uncle at Burton Agnes (or Agnes Burton), in the East Riding, but felt sure he was now living somewhere beyond Pontefract. He also went into great detail about several of the gang's 'safe houses' near Sherwood Forest at Tuxford, near Nottingham, and the eastern side of Retford, and Wentbridge, Yorkshire. In fact, Skipwith said that he, himself had ridden out to request a loan from the pockets of the extortionists' but on arrival the landlady of the inn told him that 'the birds had flown the nest'. She added that she had been paid in full for lodgings before they left the establishment. Skipwith inferred that the landlady hinted to him that they had robbed excisemen and this was how they were able to pay the bill and purchase two horses.

Since the highwaymen had gone Skipwith told the magistrates that he returned home empty handed.

## 1676 NEVISON ARRESTED

Records of York Castle inform the reader that "he (Nevison) appears to have been arrested in March 1676, but the dispositions are too imperfect to gather from them the nature of the offence with which he is charged. He was, however, condemned, but was reprieved, together with a woman named Jane Nelson." However, there was to be a happy turnaround in Nevison's fortune when out-of-necessity he found that he had to ride-for-his-life...

## 1676 THE RIDE – KENT TO YORK

Nevison's ride was remembered but was attributed erroneously for many years to another highwayman by the name of Dick Turpin. The author Baines in his Historical Directory and Gazetteer of York vol. II published in 1823 rightly accredits Nevison and his bay mare for the incredible feat.

Defoe gives the fullest and I think best account of the ride in his work entitled Defoes's Tour Through Great Britain. "From Gravesend we see nothing remarkable on the road but Gads Hill, a noted place for robbing of seamen after they have received their pay at Chatham. Here it was that the famous robbery was committed in the year 1676. It was about four o'clock in the morning when a gentleman was robbed by one Nicks, on a bay mare, just on the declining part of the hill, on the west side, for he swore to the spot and to the man. Mr. Nicks, who robbed him, come away to Gravesend, was stopped by the difficulty of the boat, and of the passage, near an hour; which was a great discouragement to him, but was a kind bait to his horse.

A relic from the past. The remaining part of Cottingley Bridge, once part of the Old North Road, now blending into the landscape.

From thence he rode across the county of Essex, through Tilbury, Hornton... to Chelmsford; here he stopped about half-an-hour to refresh his horse, and give him some balls; from thence to Braintree, Bocking, Wethersfield; then over the downs to Cambridge, and from thence, keeping still the cross roads, he went by Fenny Stanton to Godmanchester and Huntington, where he baited himself and his mare about an hour. Then, holding on the North Road, and keeping full larger gallop most of the way, he came to York the same afternoon, put off his boots and riding clothes, and went dressed as if he had been an inhabitant of the place, not a traveller, to the bowling-green, (the Bowling Green is still visible today in York Museum Gardens) where among other gentlemen was the Lord Mayor (John Ramsden) of the city; he, singling out his lordship, studied to do something particular that the mayor might remember him by, and accordingly lays some odd bet with him concerning the bowls then running, which would cause the mayor to remember it more particularly and takes occasion to ask his lordship, what o'clock it was; who pulling out his watch, told him the hour, which was quarter before, or a quarter after eight at night.

Some other circumstances, it seems be carefully brought into their discourse should make the Lord Mayor remember the day. Upon pulling a prosecution which happened afterwards for this robbery, the whole merit of this case turned upon a single point. The person robbed swore as above to the man, to the place, and to the time, in which the fact was committed, namely, that he had been robbed on Gad's Hill in Kent, on such a day, at such a time of the day, and on such a part of the hill, and the prisoner at the bar was the man who had robbed him. Nick's the prisoner, denied the facts, called several persons to his reputation, alleged that he was as far off as Yorkshire at that time, and that particularly, the day whereupon the prosecution swore he was robbed, as he was at bowls on the Public Green in the City of York; and to support this he produced the Lord Mayor of York to testify that he was so, and that the Mayor acted so and so with him there as above. This was so positive and well attested that the jury acquitted him on the bare supposition that it was impossible the man could be in two places so remote on one and the same day. There are more particulars related to this story, such as I do not take upon me to affirm; namely that the King Charles II. prevailed upon him, on assurance of pardon and that he should not be brought into any further trouble about it, to confess the truth to him privately, and that he own'd to his Majesty that he committed the robbery, and how he rode the journey after it, and that upon this the King endowed him with the soubriquet Swift Nick." How did the King come to know of Nevison's exploits? Because the robber bragged about it! After his meeting with Charles II who himself bred good English race horses, the highwayman became the hero of the hour.

The Newcastle Weekly Chronicle of the 7th March 1885 although quoting the date of 1675 gives an interesting take on the story as follows; "The main point of interest about this man Nevison now-a-days is that he was in reality the person who performed the feat traditionally attributed to Dick Turpin: (dubbed dauntless Dick) on account of the author Harrison Ainsworth in his work Rookwood that, namely riding from London to York in one day. The date cannot be precisely fixed; but it was probably in the summer of 1675. He had committed a robbery in London, just before dawn and was recognised. He made for the North at once. By sunset say 15 hours later he entered York, having ridden the one mare 200 hundred miles. There he was captured, and brought to trial, when it was proved that he had been seen on the bowling green at York on the evening of the same day and the burglary had been committed in London; and both judge and jury accepted this as a sufficient alibi, with the result that he was acquitted."

Note: June 1676 was exceptionally hot when the ride took place.

## 1606 - JOHN LEPSTONE LONDON TO YORK

Fuller's Worthies states that; John Lepstone Esq, of York for a huge wager bet James I that he could ride between Aldersgate, London to the City of York several times on consecutive days. He set off early on Monday 20th May 1606 beginning his journey from Aldersgate and arrived in York before it was dark the same evening. He did this several times in the same week and back to London. It must be said that Mr Lepstone rode a fresh horse each day of the journey, resting every ten miles or so, unlike Nevison's bay mare it is claimed to have had very little rest. Immortal Turpin by Arti Ashe and Julius E. Day published by Staples 1949 on page 137 attributes the great ride to York to neither Turpin or Nevison but to Mr Lepstone.

## MR POWELL, THE GREAT WALKER

Mr. Powell walked from London to York and back in six days. He set off on Monday 29th November 1773 and arrived in York on Wednesday afternoon of the same week.

## WHO WAS HARRIS?

A book entitled The Narrative of the Life and Surprising Robberies and Adventures of William Page published in the year 1758 claims that it was a man named Harris who in 1676, "committed a robbery in the morning in Surrey, on a gentleman who knew him perfectly well, and therefore Harris rode for it, with such speed, thrusting to the goodness of his mare, that in the evening, about sunset, he appeared on the Bowling Green at York, and pulling out his watch, showed it to the gentlemen present.

But not withstanding this prodigious performance, namely the riding of 194 miles in one day, so positive was the evidence against him that he was convicted upon it. The Old Duke of Richmond, as I remember, was so charmed with the vastness of the performance, and the bravery of the man, that he interceded for his life and obtained it..."

## WHAT ODDS?

In 1831 Nevison's epic ride from Kent to York was broken by betting man Squire George Osbaldeston, of Ebberston Hall, Malton. He was known as the "Sporting Squire of England" but only after he had changed horses twenty eight times! He did the ride in less than twelve hours. Jockey Peter Scudamore in 1993 did the same ride, changing horses forty eight times!

## COACH TRAVEL

Coach travel was a risky business before and after the days of Nevison. In summertime coaches ran between London and York and vice vera, London travellers were informed; "Whoever is desirous of going between London and York.. let them repair to The Black Swan in Holborn. Or the Black Swan in Coney Street, York, where they will be conveyed in the stagecoach if God permits, which stand every Thursday at five in the morning." Thus highwaymen would have to be up very early to catch their quarry. Times were lean for 'Jack' come winter because the coaches stopped running. Passengers submitted themselves to a very rough journey owing to the bad state of the uneven rutted roads and sometimes flooding. In 1700 it took a coach seven days to travel to London or York.

# ROOKWOOD

Harrison Ainsworth wrongly attributed Nevison's ride to the rogue Dick Turpin. At the beginning of the 1900's Ainsworth's biographer S.M. Ellis, set out to follow Turpin's (Nevison's) route from Tottenham, London to Newark thence onto the City of York. He recorded that there was not a single village alongside the Old North Road that did not have some kind of memorial of the highwayman, Turpin.

## NEVISON'S ONE- EYED MARE

As we know, the name of Nevison's brave mare remains a mystery. But it is stated that the beast was utterly devoted to its master, following him around like a pet dog to the last. The animal could single him out in a crowd like a dog. One old man claimed Nevison was adept at horsecraft and knew the secret art of horse whispering. This dusky brown coloured horse possessed but one eye and although only a three quarter thoroughbred, who might have inherited what is known as the 'speed gene' as termed by Emmerline Hill, of University College of Dublin. This mare was capable of carrying the weight of a man with sustained speed over extended distances and it was due to her fleetness and stamina that enabled the highwayman to escape his pursuers on numerous occasions.

Did Nevison employ the following 17th century method enabling his horse to cover the ground from London to York? The following article comes from Robert Greene's book of Notable Things, Page 157, No. 14.

It is certain means, upon a journey, to keep your horse, if he be of strength, and found that he shall not tire, but go on his journey's end. If he be dull, and care not for the whip or spur, alight and go to the smith's shop, and get a horse nail, and run through the horses ear, bend the sharp end of it, and let the clapper hang pretty low in his ear, which whether by sudden noise it makes in his head, or that it affrights and keeps him from heaviness, it is sure that as long as that hangs in his ear, he will go on his way.

It is my belief that King Charles II, a betting man himself, — his favourite horse being 'Old Rowley,' actually named the horse 'Swift' and Nevison, Mr. Nicks (like the devil Old Nick or 'Owd Nick') and down through the years the two names merged together becoming Swiftnicks.

### NEVISON, HORSE WHISPER

How was Nevison's mare able to single him out? According to Fairfax's The Complete Sportsman; "...to make a horse follow its master, and to find him out and challenge him amongst ever so many people. Take a pound of oatmeal, to which put a quarter of a pound of honey, and a half a pound of liquorice, make a little cake thereof, and put into your bosom next to your naked skin, then run and labour yourself till you sweat, and so rub all your sweat upon your cake; then keep the horse fasting a day and a night and give it to him to eat, which done, turn him loose, and he shall not only follow you, but also hunt and seek you out when he has lost you; and when he comes to you spit in his mouth, anoint his tongue with your spittle, and thus doing he will never forsake you."

## FALSE HEARTED LOVE

**Nevison seems to have held a fascination for many women, the old historian Scatchard in his book entitled The History of Morley said of Nevison's woman "Like a formidable Samson, he had at Dunningley, his 'Delilah' — a married woman, I believe, whose offspring and descendants (whether improperly or otherwise I know not) were long honoured with his name" Relating to Nevison and his affairs of the heart, York Castle Records state; "He was married. He was like a sailor, for he had a wife in every port." Oliver Heywood claims that Nevison "married a wife at an alehouse thereabouts" close to Howley Hall.**

## THE HIGHWAYMAN (in part)

And still of a winter's night, when the wind is in the trees,

When the moon is a ghostly galleon tossed on a cloudy sea,

When the road is a ribbon of moonlight over the     purple moor,

A highwayman comes riding — Riding-riding-

A highwayman comes riding, up to the old in door.

Over the cobbles he clattered and clashed in the dark courtyard,

And he tapped with his whip on the shutters, but all was locked and barred;

He whistled a tune at the window, and who should be waiting there

But the landlord's black eyed daughter

Bess, the landlord's daughter

Plaiting a dark red love knot into her long black hair.
Alfred Noyes first published in Blackwood's Magazine 1909

# TURN COAT

Elizabeth Burton, better known as Bess, Burton, at one-time close associate in crime, perhaps a lover or even wife of Nevison, for about two years, whom, after she was caught stealing clothes in Mansfield, Yorkshire in January 1677 was brought before Sir John Resesby, Bt, of York Assizes, on or about 3rd January. She confessed to being well acquainted with highwayman Nevison, of the County of York, and his knights-of-the-road, namely, Edmund Bracey of Nottingham (who had introduced her to Nevison), Thomas Wilbore of the same place, one Thomas Tankard of Lincoln, John Barrett (or Brommet), and Robert Everson, of no fixed abode but known at the sign of The Talbot Inn, Newark, Nevison's other headquarters, she claimed, were placed at York, Lincoln, Nottingham and Derby. She admitted that the gang hired a room at the Talbot Inn from the landlord, paid for on an annual basis. Bess confessed knowing that after each big job Nevison and his men retired to the inn to divvy up their ill-gotten gains. Bess also let slip in her statement that she too received part of the swag going on to say that somewhere twixt Grantham and Stamford, Nevison, Barrett and Everson did steal £300 from a shop keeper there. She received enough money from this haul to pay three months rent. Bess continued spilling the beans giving evidence that a hold-up took place at 'Maultby', Yorkshire, done by Nevison, Tankard and Bracey where the robbers relieved one Malim of Rotherham, of £200 on the road to Gainsbrough. In Lincolnshire the men netted a great amount of riches by means of robbery. After this Bess seemed unwilling or unable to provide further information excepting she added, when Nevison, Bracey, Wilbore and Tankard committed a further robbery where they made £300 of which Bess admitted she received 34 shillings (£3.40 pence). She had fritted the money on one white and one serge petticoat and two bodices. Bess also stated there was one last robbery she knew about which took place at Royston, just prior to her arrest committed by the whole gang she had previously named in deposition. This took place, she stated, between May Day and Lammas last. The proceeds of this raid amounted to £250 which included both gold and silver. She had done rather well out of it receiving two gold pieces and enough in silver to pay six months lodging with £2 10s 8p left over. Bess Burton had purchased more clothes with the money. She swore too that the landlord of the Talbot Inn, Newark, was in the thick of it, taking his own "cut" from the robberies. She also claimed that the inn's ostler, William Anwood, took bribes from the Nevison gang to secretly "keep their horses close and never to water them but night time."Note: Records of York Castle gives the woman's name as Mary Burton and that she was employed as a housekeeper by the gang.

## PENAL TRANSPORTATION

Robert Holgate was in dire need of a horse in February 1677. Nevison was more than happy to oblige, offering him a distinctive dapple gray horse. Mr Holgate, liking the horse, decided to test it. Riding through the town of Barnsley, the true owner, Pontefact man, Jeremiah Peele recognised his missing gelding. Robert Holgate was questioned on 9th February and Nevison was arrested for stealing Mr Peele's horse at the York Assizes about a month later. He was also charged with having robbed a purse near Wombwell. Apparently, after a search of his widowed mother's home in Wortly, the purse, or wallet was discovered hidden behind a chest. Nevison was convicted on both counts, receiving a pardon only on condition that he would promise to inform upon his accomplices-in-crime.

## 1681 BREAKS LOOSE

After receiving his reprieve from the justices, he refused to inform against any of his comrades, and was still incarcerated in York gaol in the July of 1681. He was finally drafted into Captain Graham's Company based in Tangier on the North African coast. The 1681 Records from Wakefield House of Correction tell us that Nevison managed to stage yet another daring escape in 1681 from York Castle — most probably aided by his cohorts. The records state that; "Sir John Reresby... the last governor of York, when John Nevison broke loose..." was extremely angry.

Until the time of Nevison's covert departure from York Castle, it was believed that there was not one man alive who could escape from this prison, so impregnable were its thick stone walls. Many people in the land looked up to Nevison, and to mark this feeling many songs and ballads were written about his antics, whether they be true or false. Hero or not, Sir John Reresby personally petitioned King Charles II on 23rd October 1681 (for a second time?). Telling the King that Nevison had again escaped and that the highwayman had "lately committed several notorious robberies in the district and it was only "with great endeavours and trouble that I got him apprehended at first; and since his escape he has threatened the death of several justices, whenever he met them; though I never heard that I was one of their number."

The king being no real admirer of his courtesan Reresby, and having a liking for Nevison, at first refused to issue a proclamation saying to do so would cost him £100. In the end a compromise was struck between the two men and it was agreed that £20 would be offered as the reward since this would be paid not by the king but by the Sheriff of the county that took the missing robber. A warrant went out for the arrest of Nevison, a robber, horse stealer who escaped from York Castle and "rideth arm'd to the terror of the king's evidence and the jury and the encouragement of lewd people." The warrant is still in existence and is held by West Yorkshire Archives, ref; Wakefield QSI/20/9 Oct 1681. Although Reresby was later to claim in his memoirs that Nevison was taken soon after nobody came forward to claim the cash and the highwayman was free to wander at will without fear until the advent of Darcy Fletcher some three years later.

## LEICESTER JAIL- PLAGUE-DARING ESCAPE

In no time at all Nevison appears to have fallen foul of the law and arrested yet again. This time in the centre of England, where he was taken to Leicester prison. Nevison was able to affect a means of escape aided by his friends in 1681. How may you ask did he manage to do this? Clapped in heavy leg irons and fetted to a cell wall? Nevison feigned the symptoms of having the plague. Knowing full well a medical man would be called without delay a friend of his pretended to be a doctor. It was this 'medical doctor' that advised the prison governor that Nevison had contracted the plague. The prisoner was instantly removed away from the vicinity of the other inmates to a room on his own.

The jailer's wife forbade her husband to go near Nevison for fear that he too should catch the infectious disease. So both men had a clear run in order to concoct a liberation plan. And it was a very cunning plan indeed.

It entailed the 'doctor' visiting his patient several times a day. Later a second opinion was called for and the 'doctor' brought in a man to covertly paint Nevison's body with blue looking spots, mimicking the symptoms of the bubonic plague! A few days later the 'doctor' called to see his patient and after slipping Nevison a strong sleeping draught the 'doctor' pronounced the highwayman dead!

A Coroner's jury at the inquest, afraid to venture close to the corpse of a plague victim for absolute fear of catching the dreaded illness themselves. After seeing the spots of and marks of death about him, his eyes set, and his jaws muffled, decreed the prisoner dead of the plague. Nevison's 'corpse' was instantly carted away from the prison in a rough coffin, by his victorious friends. Once more Nevison had escaped justice, having outwitted the hangman and the hangman's noose!

"Being thus discharged, he fell to his former trade again, and meeting several of his old tenants, the carriers, who used to pay him rents, (the insurance trick) told them they must advance the same, as his last imprisonment had cost him a great sum of money, which he expected to be reimbursed among them. They being strangely surprised at the sight of Mr Nevison, reported about that his ghost walked, and took upon it the employment he was wont when he was living. This was confirmed by the gaoler at Leicester, who had brought in the verdict of the jury on oath, who had examined the body, and found it dead; whereby he had been discharged by the court, as to the warrant of his commitment. When the same came to be known, and the cheat detected, the gaoler was ordered to fetch him in at his peril." Nevison decided to return to his own country in the North to continue in his old ways.

After it became known Nevison had duped everyone at the Leicester Prison an order was issued for his arrest. Yet another proclamation for a sum amounting to £20 was offered for his early capture nevertheless he was to remain a free man for several more years.

It is easy to see how Nevison was able to use the fear of plague for it had been a very odd year weather wise as the parish registers of Alstonfield record that in the month of December 1680, " a very strange and fiery meteor in the image of a sword appeared in the north-west, west sky, (known as Kirch's Comet)." The meteor held its position for more than six weeks-well into 1681. On April 10th there came a long dry season, which ended on June 20th. Also, that: " Many pestileutions, diseases as argues, strong fevers, cum multis aliis (with many others) smallpox... Many died in towns and cities that year." No wonder then, that nobody, would touch the supposed plague 'corpse' of the highwayman.

## MOON MEN

Making good his escape from Leicestershire, Nevison headed towards London On the way met with a band of villains. It amused him to spend a little time with the gypsys (known as moon men), they unwittingly entertaining the King of all robbers. Nevison asked if he could enter into their "honourable fraternity?" Their leader replied: "Do we not come into the world arrant beggars', without a rag upon us? And do we not go out of the world like beggars', saving a sheet over us?

Shall we then, be ashamed to walk up and down the world, like beggars', with old blankets pinned about us? No, no, that would be a shame to us, indeed. Have we not the whole kingdom to walk in at our pleasure? Are we afraid at the approach of quarter day? Do we walk in fear of Sheriffs, bailiffs, and catchpoles? Whosoever knew an errant beggar arrested for debt? Does not every man's cellar afford us beer, and the best men's purses keep a penny for us to spend? Nevison upon hearing these eloquent words from the clapperdogeon (a beggar born and bred) made his mind up there and then to become one of their number... at least whilst it amused him to do so.... His membership cost him eighteen pence which was immediately spent on best beer to celebrate his initiation to the gang. Nevison was ordered to kneel down, and whilst kneeling he was promptly baptized with a quart pot of ale poured over his head by the chief of beggars who at the same time declared; "I do by virtue of this sovereign liquor, install thee in the Roage, (an insulting word) and make thee a free denizen of our ragged regiment. Henceforth, it shall be lawful to cant, (canting being a secret language of thieves) only observing these rules: - First, that thou art not to wander up and down all countries, but to keep to that quarter that is allocated to thee; and, secondly, thou art to give away to any of us that have borne all the officers of the wallet before; and, upon holding up a finger, to avoid any town or country village where thou see est we are foraging for victuals for our army that marches along with us. Observing these two rules, we take thee under our protection, and constitute thee a brother of our numerous society.

The band of brothers shouted so much that the ceremony

was halted until complete silence was restored. The chief continued: - "Now that thou art entered into our fraternity, thou must not scruple to act any villainies, whether it be cut or purse, steel a cloak-bag or portmanteau, convey all manner of things, whether they be chickens, suckling pigs, ducks, geese, or hens; or to steal a shirt from the hedge; for he that will be a queer cove (meaning a professional rogue) must adhere to the following rules; And because thou art but a novice in begging and understand not the mysteries of the canting language, thou shalt have a wife to be thy companion, from whom thou mayest receive instruction." A seventeen-year-old girl was duly selected to be Nevison's wife and they were wed there and then by the offices of a gypsy priest. A hen's head was cut off. The remains were placed on the floor on each side of the bride and groom. This done the priest said in a raised voice that the pair should live together until death parted them. The happy couple held hands and kissed — thus sealing the pact they had made to one another. The evening was spent in a jovial atmosphere and everyone got drunk and when the last drop had gone and the rabble obliged to sleep it off John Nevison made another escape under the cover of darkness! Sadly history does not record the fate of his vagabond bride.

## NEVISON REFUSES TO ROB OLD WOMAN

From the pages William Smith's Old Yorkshire published in 1883 comes this Nevison tale; "In connection with the widow of "John Green, Junr., late of Liversedge Hall, subdued to Mortalls fate" we find that at Leeds Sessions,

**in 1681, Robert Mellor, of Liversedge, was accused at the Leeds Sessions of an attempt to rob Mrs. Mary Greene, widow, of Liversedge Hall of £400. He confessed the plot; the noted John Nevison the highwayman, and his brother Stephen (is there a brother of this name?) Nevison had refused to assist him. "**

Lower Hall Liversedege, residence of the Green Family.

## PART TWO: THE BIRD IS IN THE CAGE
## DARK AND DEADLY DEED AT HOWLEY

Woodkirk Fair, afterwards known as Lee Fair in Nevison's day, harked way back to the days of Henry Ist. The country fair was held two days before the Feast of the nativity of Mary and on the feast day itself. The dates were the 13th to 15th of August and again on 6th to 8th of September each year.

As was Nevison's custom when visiting Lee Fair, being near Howley, he stayed at the local inn whose landlord was Darcy Fletcher, who had been a long time friend of his, having saved his neck on at least several counts. But on this occasion Darcy, together with his brother planned to reap the £20 reward set for their friend's capture, as sealed by Royal Proclamation. With easy money foremost in mind, the two kinsmen, having made their cunning plan, welcomed the unsuspecting Nevison with open arms. After the highwayman had given over his horse to the inn's ostler, and settled himself down; Darcy Fletcher filled a large pot with drugged ale. The smiling turncoat set it down onto a rough hewn table and waited for the effects of the drug to take hold.... However, the plan backfired, when Nevison came round sooner than calculated to find he had been locked in an upstairs chamber. As he was affecting his escape via the window the following morning, he was accosted by Darcy Fletcher, who let fly, doing his best to overpower him, but since Nevison was equally bent on escape they fought each other, and in the heat of the moment, the highwayman's flintlock pistol went off, accidently killing Darcy Fletcher stone dead (villagers claimed that it was not a pistol that ended Fletcher's life, but a bloody dagger, which was later retrieved from the thatch of a cottage close to where the fight took place).

Yorkshire Stories Retold by James Burnley 1890 relates a different version of events; "Finding himself again overcome by force, Nevison had recourse to a 'bosom friend' — a short pistol, which firing at the heart of Fletcher, he rolled, from his body a lifeless corpse."

Quickly, retrieving the key to the stable from the dead man's pocket, Nevison sprang out of the window, alighted onto a heap of manure below, saddled his mare which had been fastened within, and headed out towards the village of Morley, and from here onto York, followed closely by Fletcher's brother, calling for him to surrender himself. Nevison turned, quoting treachery and ingratitude on the brothers' part. After Fletcher's death Nevison, aware that he was now truly a marked man, actually disguised himself in order to evade capture. For Nevison this was to be the beginning of the end for not only was he a wanted thief but now he was a murderer too. He could have slipped out of the country, assumed a false identity, and quietly gone to ground abroad. This would have been fairly easy thing to achieve in those days. Instead he chose to stay and take his chances....

Note; If Lee Fair was held in only August and September each year, then Nevison must have killed Fletcher in 1683, and have evaded arrest for several months prior to his arrest.

## FLETCHER GRAVEMARKER

In a lonely spot, close to a large wood, overlooking the town of Batley, close to the ruins of old Howley Hall with its resident female spectre once stood a small roughly hewn stone carved by the hand of "Trash" Jackson. The words were simple but served the passerby as a reminder of the murder committed by Nevison on that fateful day in 1683 it read; HERE NEVISON KILLED FLETCHER

Scatchard in his work entitled The History of Far Famed Howley Hall near Batley, Yorkshire gives an account of where this memorial stone could be located, he says; "About one hundred yards from the farmhouse at Howley, on the west side, and near to the footpath to Morley, lies a small stone of cylindrical shape, bearing the above inscription. This stone was cut and engraved by John Jackson, the schoolmaster of Lee Fair, commonly called "Old Trash." The stone was sunk into the ground at the very spot where Fletcher took a bullet into his heart. This memorial was scarcely legible in the latter part of the 1800's. A newspaper report dated 2nd February 1953 claimed that the ghost of Nevison has often been seen close to the site of the murder. Witnesses have also reported hearing him too.

## LOOK UPON A TRAITOR - THE NET TIGHTENS

Nevison was now running for his life. Perhaps hush money may have saved him from the gallows, but in the end, and, even though it was a Leap Year, he was betrayed by a woman.

It was well known that the fugitive Nevison, used an inn standing between Castle Terrace and Manygates Lane, Sandal, near Wakefield, (opposite its replacement, The Three Houses, at 379, Barnsley Road, Sandal, Wakefield) where at that time it there were three different inns. The Magpie, The Crossed Keys and The Plough.

The Sign of the 'Three Houses' Sandal, near Wakefield, Yorkshire. Swift Nick was finally captured near here at the 'Magpie' in 1684

The former inn known as The Magpie was kept by a woman known to share her bed with the highwayman. The landlady was offered the sum of ten guineas by the Constable of Sandal, a Captain Hardcastle (only about half the reward offered in a public notice). If she promised to inform on her lover the next time he called at the inn. And so it was that on 6th March 1684 the landlady turned traitor, and unable to turn down the chance of easy money, sent a cryptic message to Captain Hardcastle. It read; "Sir-The bird is in the cage." The receiver knew exactly what this meant and hastily summoned help in the form of Mr J Ramsden and together with others set off to the inn from whence the message had come.

The reward notice in the London Gazette ran for three days, beginning 27th of October 1683, offering a reward of £20 to anyone for the arrest of Nevison. The notice read;

> Nevison, hath lately murdered Fletcher, who had a warrant to apprehend him...'

Knowing this the men went fully armed with braces of Queen Anne pistols. Hardcastle carried a signed warrant for the fugitives' arrest. It was about the hour of midnight when he and his men arrived at Sandal and Nevison was taken into custody after being discovered in a locked upper bed chamber, sound asleep in an armchair. Having broken into the room the miscreant was arrested and taken forcefully from the inn, leaving his precious horse behind.

Hunter's Additional M.S. document set's out the case thus; "Upon Thursday, March 6$^{th}$ 1684, one Mr J. Hardcastle, of Penthorp, near Wakefield, understanding that Mr John Nevison, the highwayman, was drinking at the alehouse near Sandal Castle, took someone with him, and so apprehended and brought him to Wakefield.

Mr White made him a mittimus, and sent him to York in the midst of the Assizes..." (Mittimus was the name of an order in writing, issued from a Court enabling a Sheriff or other officer "to receive and safely keep the person until his or her fate shall be determined by the due course of law."

However, Scatchard the historian quotes quite a different version of events in which he says that it was a valiant tailor who "finding him (Nevison) asleep on a bench.., pinioned his arms and procured assistance.

This is thought to have been the chair occupied by Nevison on the night of his capture by Captain Hardcastle and the others.

Official records do not back up Scatchard's statement for it is recorded in Wakefield Session's dated 9th October 1684, (several months after the capture of Nevison) that an "Order for the constable of Sandal to pay John Ramsden the sum of ten shillings and six pence....for conveying one Nevison, a highwayman, to the Castle of York..." Hardcastle and Ramsden were also paid 2s 6d for getting the mittimus. The journey in total took three days to complete. Nevison must have been well guarded rendering him unable to escape his captors' although they may have stopped along the way at one of Nevison's watering holes at Swinnington Bridge (known as Sinnington) at the sign of the Black Swan for a sup of ale.

Writing in 1745 Arthur Jessop recorded the passing of a Mr Hardcastle, late of Wakefield whose grandfather had arrested Nevison, during one of the coldest winters on record.

### BEWARE THE IDES OF MARCH

As Nevison stood before the court (the same Assizes which condemned Jennet Preston, one of the famous Pendle Witches, in 1612), no new indictment was preferred against him, only the clerk asked him what he had to say about why he believed execution should not be done to him, according to a former sentence. Nevison replied that he could not be killed for he had the King's pardon - a reprieve from his former sentence. He went on to explain that he had gone as an ensign into one of His Majesty's Foot Companies to Tangier, but having got there, fell ill for three months, after which his captain went abroad and because of his illness he found he was unable to follow his regiment. The judge listened carefully to the prisoner's tale, but felt he had no choice, but to reactivate the outstanding conviction from a previous trial back in 1677, even though he had received a pardon against his former death sentence, the pardon was conditional. Nevison having deserted his regiment, had forfeited his life in the process, and because of his actions the original conviction must stand. The judge told the court; "he must dye for he was a terror to the country" then pronounced sentence...." And so it was that the highwayman's, date with death by way of slow strangulation, at the end of a rope, and was fixed for Saturday March 15$^{th}$ 1683-4 – the same day on which Julius Caesar met his death.

## MOURNFUL WORDS OF A BELLMAN

The following text featuring in the Introduction of Captain Alexander Smith's Lives of the Highwaymen, 1719 gives an excellent insight of a felon's last days on earth.

"...while warrants were being signed the bellman...would cry aloud, in doleful tones, his solemn exhortation:

>    You the prisoner that are within.

>    Who for wickedness and sin,

After many mercies shewn you, are now appointed to die tomorrow in the forenoon, Give ear and understanding that tomorrow morning the bell... shall toll for you, in form and manner of a passing bell , as used to be tolled for those that are at the point of death, to the end that all godly people hearing that bell, and knowing that it is for you going to your death(s), may be stirred up heartily to pray to God to bestow his grace and mercy upon you while you live. I beseech you, for Jesus Christ, his sake, to keep this night in watching and prayer for the salvation of your own soul(s), while there is yet time and place for mercy, as knowing to-morrow you must appear before the Judgement Seat of your Creator, there to give an account of all things done in this life; and to suffer eternal torments for your sins committed against him, unless upon your hearty and unfeigned repentance, you find mercy, through the merits, death and passion of your only Mediator and Advocate, Jesus Christ, who now sits at the right hand of God, to make intercession for as many of you as penitently return to him."

Frenchman, Francis Misson, paints for us in full colour warts and all, the final journey of a condemned soul. In 1698 he writes:

"They put five or six in a cart (some gentlemen obtain leave to perform this journey in a coach), and carry them, riding backwards with the rope about their necks, to the fatal tree. The executioner stops the cart under one of the cross beams of the gibbet, and fastens to that ill-favoured beam one end of the rope, while the other is wound round the wrench's neck. This done, he gives the horse a lash with his whip, away goes the cart, and there swing my gentlemen kicking in the air. The hangman does not give himself the trouble to put them out of their pain; but some of their friends or relations do it for them. They pull the dying person by the legs, and beat his breast to despatch him as soon as possible. The English are people that laugh at the delicacy of other nations who make it such a mighty matter to be hanged; their extraordinary courage looks upon it as a trifle, and they also make a jest of the pretended dishonour that, in the opinion of others, falls upon their kindred.
He that is hanged or otherwise executed first takes care to get himself shaved and handsomely dressed, either in the morning, or in the dress of a bridegroom. This done, he sets his friends at work to get him leave to be buried, and to carry his coffin with him, which is easily obtained. When his suit of clothes, or (woollen) night-gown, his gloves, hat, periwig, nosegay, coffin, flannel dress for his corpse, and all these things are bought and prepared, the main point is taken care of, his mind is at peace and then he thinks of his conscience. Generally he studies a speech, which he pronounces under the gallows, and gives in writing to the sheriff or to the minister that attends him in his last moments, desiring that it may be printed."

In the early hours of the fatal morning Nevison's cart would have come to the prison yard to collect him. He would have kitted himself out in the best outfit (he liked the best in life, following the fashion of the day) and the best coffin he could afford.

The noose was placed about his neck before setting off. The procession followed a well trod road that led to York's Knavesmire gallows, stopping no doubt at the last inn along the way. It was the custom that a condemned person was given ale (known as The Cup of Charity originating from the time of King Henry 1). The nearest inn to the gallows, was usually known as 'The Last Drop.'

## DEATH COME, QUICKLY AWAY!

One can only guess what was running through the mind of Nevison on the appointed day of his execution, a very cold day. Did he hope for a reprieve at the last moment? The Nevison motto is; Where there is life, there is hope. Could he affect some other means of escape as he did on previous occasions? No, it was not to be, for Nevison's hour glass had at last run dry. Released from his fetters and pair of leg irons at the last moment, Nevison found he was to be the only star turn that day. Dutifully joining the priest in prayer and singing a psalm, after which he delighted a huge crowd of ghoulish onlookers by entertaining them with his well-prepared farewell speech as he stood perched upon the gallows ladder waiting to be launched into eternity. What follows is the text of Nevison's supposed rendition, according to a published tract of the day which began;

"Good people, I now freely confess to you all, that for my Sins and Enormities, the judgement of GOD, the Law of the Kingdom, and the equity of my Sentence, have brought me here to suffer Punishment, I forgive all the World, as I hope those whom I have injured, will forgive me the least true Content of Mind. As King David saith. There is No Peace for the Wicked; so a Robber is continually restless, whether riding, walking, eating, waking or sleeping; Frightful Dreams disturb him, daily crimes fill up the measure of his iniquities, till at length he finds himself involved in Despair.

But the greatest Crime that troublesome, which upon my panting Heart seems to like to a ponderous Mountain of Lead, is the Death of Mr Fletcher, because I never murdered a Person before; and I now wish he had rather taken my Life than his, tho' it was my own Defence, I hope that my ignominious Death will strike terror into Wicked Person, as well as others who hear my Fate, as those who see me die. Disobedience to Parents, Contempt of Superiors, and neglect of the Lord's Day, led me insensibly into Temptation. My Gallantry in giving to the Poor, I know had been applauded, but we can in no way excuse my taking from the Rich; who tho' they enjoy great Store of Wealth, have equal Care to balance their felicity, I am willing to leave this transitory Stage. I depart praying for you all; desiring your Prayers, as you behold me expiring, that my Departing Soul may be wash'd in the purest streams proceeding from the Eternal Fountain of Mercy, Come Lord JESU! Receive my sorrowful Spirit. In Thee I trust, let me not, in my last Moments, be confounded."

Was this truly Nevison's swan song? or as Samuel Pepys noted; The Hangman's Advice or Nevison's Last Legacy to the Knight's of the high-pad, published 1684. However, other sources of the day claim that the highwayman was blind drunk at the end, incapable of saying anything coherent having had too much of the 'last drop' before facing the 'short drop.'

Perhaps Nevison was telling the truth that his short barrelled flintlock, did go off accidentally? And that the already loaded half-cocked gun's safety catch somehow got released during the fierce struggle between Nevison and the dead man. Whatever the truth of the matter, his story was not believed by the judge nor the jury.

## MYSTERY OF INN AND NEVISON'S CHATTELS

Captain Alex Smith, in his book, A Complete History of the Lives and Robberies of the most Notorious Highwaymen and Footpads, Shoplifts and Cheats of both Sexes. 1719, gives an interesting account of what a prisoner might expect if he did not admit to his crime.

"The Press Yard was actually an exercise ground, where the punishment of peine fort et dure, or pressing to death, was administered to those who stood mute at their trial and refused to plead Guilty or Not Guilty. The incentive to such stoicism was that the goods of one who refused to plead could not be forfeited to the Crown nor, in the case of a thief, be given to the informers who brought about his apprehension. The thief or highwayman, who could withstand the agony to the end, his body crushed but not his determination, thus left the proceeds of his villainy to his family and escaped making any restitution. There were not so many possessed of such fortitude. One culprit, a highwayman, bore a weight of 350lb. On his chest for half an hour rather than that his mare should fall into strange hands, but when another 50lb. Piece of lead was added to the burden, he could stand the pain no longer, and yielded. He was tried, sentenced, and hanged, and the mare for which he suffered so much was, by a cruel cynicism of the Law, given to the man who had turned evidence against her master. This form of punishment was abolished so late as 1772." Captain Hardcastle's family eventually gave the chair Nevison was found sitting in to St. Helen's Church, Sandal Magna, situated not far from day's The Three Houses.

The Royalist Rector Joseph Wood (?) decreed; "from that moment only the holiest person would sit in that chair." The well worn, 17$^{th}$ century carved chair with arm and foot rest, remains in the church to this day. During the vicariate of Canon R. N. Hurt, circa 1879 — 1909, Bishop Stratton, when he was Vicar of Wakefield, gave his nephew, the Sandal vicar and wardens, for their use, a companion chair to Nevison's relic of the same size and style, which he had especially carved in Wakefield.

Under English law the Captain, was entitled to lay claim to all of Nevison's possessions, since he confessed before dying on the gallows — namely, that he did kill Fetcher, but only in self-defence. Since Hardcastle obviously got the chair, did he also claim Nevison's treasured mare?

Over the years there has been much confusion as to which inn Nevison was discovered by Hardcastle and his men. For this reason I think it is worth quoting a Yorkshire historian who visited the site and found that that "on the south corner of Castle Lane used to stand The Magpie which was turned into three cottages after being deprived of its licence when I was on a visit to Sandal in 1903. I found one of these Magpie cottages inhabited by the church sexton. The Plough, Magpie and Cross Keys appear to have been lumped together at the junction of Castle Lane, all clamouring for custom and trying to outrival each other. When the Plough and the Magpie were reduced to cottage dwellings, their licences were transferred to the Cross Keys and this triple business connection is today seen in the unusual appellation of The Three Houses on the sign of the former Crossed Keys." The same writer also suggests that there was no "authority for quoting the Magpie Inn as the house where he (Nevison) was betrayed: Sandal folk in general believe it was The Plough, a rather large, old fashioned farmhouse situated at the south corner of Castle Lane, probably where now stands the attractive residence of Yulecroft.

## REV. HEYWOOD'S THOUGHTS ON NEVISON

Extract from Oliver Heywood's Diary Vol. 4. 1630-1702; "Rampered into the net, and their precious souls tormented in hell to all eternity, this is the wages of sin, this is the fruit of which abominable courses... but shame shall be the promotion of fools, a shameful death, it may be promotion to the gallows in their uppermost preferment, this poor man at last found and confest that his Sabbath — breaking, drinking, lewd company, and courses had brought him to that shameful end, it's said he (Nevison) was a papist and had his pardon in his bosom. Oh! that all his thievish and drinking companions might learn by his example to leave their wicked ways and fear God! His time is come, and he is gone to eternity, their time will certainly, may suddenly come, little did he think that morning of the day whereon he was taken what that day would bring forth, but the text saith, he being oft reproved and hardeneth his neck shall suddenly be destroyed, and that without remedy; there is no remedy, Satan's martyrs are numerous and adventurous, they will on though they see death before them... to see thieves dying to gratify a lust,... a malefactor as if he were a wild boar, or a furious beast that devours the country, everyone rejoyeth at his fall, that justice is executed and such villains rid out of the way, and the Devil glad to see them."

Perhaps Heywood should have added;

## QUALIS VITA, FINIS ITA
## As he lived, so he died

For all of Heywood's harsh words against Nevison, it was well noted that; "In spite of his criminal ways the highwayman had a softer side to his character. He was gentle towards women and the aged, and it was written after his death that he gave liberally to those in need. He was a staunch Royalist and would never rob those loyal to the King. Gent's chapbook dated 4$^{th}$ May 1685 tells us; "This was the end of a remarkable man, Nevison, who was a person of quick understanding, tall in stature, every way proportional, exceeding valiant, having an air and carriage of a gentleman."

Note: In Victorian times it was still a common thing to hear a child's mother calling a naughty child a "Regular Nevison" in Yorkshire.

### BURIAL

Originally there had been a gibbet at Knavesmire, York until it was removed and replaced by the gallows in the year 1371. The last hanging took place in 1801 and the gallows finally dismantled in 1812. There were many such gallows in York. Nevison, did not have to worry about having his remains exposed in a metal gibbet such as the one diarist Samuel Pepys commented upon in his diary. He wrote: "Shooter's Hill. It was long the notorious haunt of highwaymen. The custom was to leave the bodies of criminals hanging until the bones fell to the ground and it was a filthy sight to see how the flesh stuck to the bones..."

Nevison's corpse was supposed to have been conveyed to St. Mary's Church, Castlegate, York where it was buried deep in a nameless grave on 16th March 1684, a day after the hanging. The ground was still hard, since there had been a great frost between mid December and January 1684, when the River Thames had frozen right up to London Bridge! By mid February there came a slight thaw.

Other sources have claimed that the highwayman was really interred in consecrated ground in the village of Haxby, near York. I do not know how this story came about, but Nevison's interment is listed in St. Mary's church records. There is one mystery though – where was Nevison's corpse between 15th and 16th March? Was his coffin taken off to a local inn, to lie in 'state' giving his family and friends the opportunity to a glass in his honour, wishing him adieu?

After Death Comes Judgment (sic) (inscription, St. Mary's Church, York)

Today, his grave remains unidentified in the Castlegate graveyard. St. Mary's was deconsecrated by the relevant authorities in 1958. The churchyard according to John Speed's map of 1610 was a much larger area than it is today, so as then, Nevison remains just as elusive, even unto the grave ...

### YORK CASTLE PRISON

York Castle was once a military garrison and later it became a county prison. According to John Howard in

Notes on York Prison 1774 the prison contained four condemned cells within the Debtors' Prison. Each cell measured about seven feet square and was close to the prison sewers which very often reeked. The only comfort was straw which was used for prisoners bedding and the only water provided had to be brought in by the jailer's servant. The leg iron's weighed 28lbs and can be viewed today in the cells at York.

The original county courts where Nevison was tried were erected in 1673 but were demolished to make way for new courts in 1777. The prison at York Castle in Nevison's day was actually much smaller until 1821 when it was afterwards remodelled.

# THE WORTLEY'S OF WORTLEY HALL

An account of Nevison's life would not be complete without looking at the history of the Wortley family who lived in such close proximity to the Nevison family. It is easy to see how a young impressionable and intelligent boy such as Nevison might have been fascinated by the life of heroic Sir Francis Worley (1591-1652). The more I read about the Baronet, the further intrigued I became, because I could see traits in Nevison akin to Royalist Sir Francis Wortley! It would not take a great leap of imagination to believe that Nevison could have easily been the illegitimate child of Sir Worley! Now read on;

1727-28 Hobson writes; "At Pilley. There was there Mr. Skelton, who has been game-keeper to the Wortley's for above 60 years. . He was born in the year 1642. He knew old Sir Francis Wortley who got the battle at Tankersley moor. He was afterwards taken prisoner (June 1644) by the Parliamentry forces, and escorted to Wolton hall, (Walton House, between Sandal Magna and Crofton, near Wakefield, Seat of the Knightly family of Waterton) by Sir Thomas Fairfax, known as 'Black Tom' and was put in the Tower of London, (on the 22$^{nd}$ August 1644, released 1649) where he died, (in 1652, at his lodgings at Whitefriars, Fleet Street, London) and was (supposedly) buried at Westminster. He was a tall proper man, with grey hair and one of the first who took up arms for the king.

This Mr Skelton, when he was about eight years, went into the service of young Sir Francis Wortley, (Sir Francis Wortley's legitimate son) who lived at St. Hellen Wells, nigh Monkbretton, having for some time before resided beyond the sea, but was permitted to come back by

Parliament upon the death of his father, whom he had disoblieged upon this account. There was a certain man call'd Bailie, of Dodsworth, who by the Commission of Array had been pressed into the king's service, this man deserted, and was retaken; whereupon young Sir Francis, without any trial by a court-martiall, caused him to be hang'd upon a tree near Wortley Hall (in other words, Wortley murdered him). Old Sir Francis was so much displeased at his son for so rash an action, that, to avoid his anger, he went to Italy, and stayed there till his father's death.

When Sir Francis, the younger (born 1616) returned, he set up stables and became a well-known horse breeder. He is believed to have owned the famous racehorse, 'Old Montagu.' Sir Francis, the younger, "had no legitimate issue by his lady, (Frances Faunt) but left a naturall daughter by a Mrs Newcommen, called, Penelope (or Ann born around 1659.)" In his will of 13th March 1665-6, Sir Francis Wortley bequeathed the whole of the estate to his illegitimate daughter. Oddly, none of the family contested his will. Having "died at Turnham green, nigh London, where he had a fine seat, and was buried at Westminster. He was a little lean man, with yellowish hair, drunk very hard, and seem'd to me melancolick, and troubled in mind..."

Note: Mrs. Newcommen (Newcome ) was actually only a child of 14 years when she gave birth to Wortley's daughter knwon as Ann.

## NEVISON'S REAL FATHER?

Oxford graduate, Sir Francis Wortley the elder; was knighted by James Ist, and afterwards made a Baronet. A true Caverlier, he was one of the earliest knights to come forward to fight for Charles Ist and later, supported Charles II. He turned his stately home, Wortly Hall, with its many secret passages, and hiding places into a fortress, setting up a Loyalist garrison of 150 infantry men during the time of Charles Ist. He became a Colonel in the 5th regiment on foot, which were a 1000 strong, and fought for the king's cause in Staffordshire, Derbyshire and in his native Yorkshire. Insulting Lord Saville, he made up with him, after challenging him to a duel in 1628. Sir Francis was to remain a firm Royalist until death. He married twice, and fathered two legitimate children, to his first wife Grace, a son, Francis, who bore no resemblance to his father, and daughter Margaret,

Was Sir Francis the elder also known as plain Frank Wortley, really Nevison's true father? If he had sired him out-of-wedlock, it would have been common practice to induce a man by bribery or other means, to marry the mother-to-be. Perhaps he persuaded his steward, John Nevison aged about 20 years old, at that time, to wed the unfortunate girl in 1638. What is interesting is that Nevison the child was also, tall of stature, and well proportioned, like Sir Francis, which was fairly unusual at the time. Gent's chapbook dated 4th May 1685 describes Nevison, the highwayman apart from being tall in stature; "exceedingly valiant, having the air and carriage of a gentleman."

Oliver Heywood said of the elder Sir Francis; "...Wortley in the time of war kept Pennistone Church as a garrison for the king... though it did him no good, but from thence he roved up and down the country, robbing and taxing many honest people." Nevison did likewise. Sir Francis left a good deal of money to the poor in his will, but his wishes were never honoured.

According to Mr Skelton, Nevison was actually living at St. Helen Wells, the home of Sir Francis the younger (possibly his half brother?) This must have been somewhere between the years of 1660-1665. Why was Nevison in residence? Nevision was also said to have an "uncle at Agnes Burton" (or Burton Agnes) whom he had resided, could this have been the home of Sir Henry Griffith who married Margaret, Sir Francis Wortley's daughter?

Strange how Nevison, a true loyalist and adventurer himself, followed in old Sir Francis's footsteps... all coincidence perhaps! If Sir Francis was not Nevison's true father then he ought to have been!

### ST HELEN WELLS IN THE PARISH OF ROYSTONE

John Hobson's dairy, dated 1727-28 sets out a particularly interesting story of an ancient farmstead, St Helen (Hellen) Wells, Yorkshire. His account tells how Nevison, having retired from the road around 1660, occupied the building for some time, along with Sir Francis Wortley jnr, Mr Skelton, gamekeeper and other servants, perhaps including Mr Nevison snr?

"At St. Helen wells (near Monkbretton) there was a room called the yellow chamber, thro' which, if any one attempted to carry a candle in the night, it would turn blue (some would say that this was the sign of a dead relative or loved one close by) and go out immediately; and over the kitchin there was an open gallery, and this Mr Skelton, as he has sate by the fire, has often seen the apparition of a boy and a girl walk along the gallery. This house is now pulled down, and lately rebuilded by Mr Sydney Wortley, for a habitation for a mistress of his, Mrs Grace Bingley, who now resides there. At the same time, there lived with this Skelton... Nevison, who afterwards was an exciseman; (at Barnsley, 2 miles north of the St Helen Wells farmhouse) but, being put out of his place, became a highwayman... At the same time there lived there a young woman, mother to the present dame Walker, of Pilley, one Wood, of Burton Smithies, made love to her; whereupon two of Sir Francis Wortley's servants (one of them call'd Lapish) quarrelled with him, and one of them clove Wood's head with a spade; (murdered him) in the court of St. Hellen's. They were sent to York, and, at the intercession of Sir Francis, came of (got off). It is said that they pretended Wood was attempting to ravish her, so they cleared themselves by saying that what they did was in defence of the young woman. This Skelton was quarter-master to a private troop which was raised to quench, the Farnley wood plot, (October 1663) and assisted at the taking of... Oates and Greathead...

He went along with his master to Exeter, where he met the Prince of Orange, who thanked Mr Wortley, for the good service he had done at York, and promised to see him paid.

This Skelton is now 86 years old, is very hearty, and rides about to look after the game in Mr Edward Wortley's liberty."

The old farmhouse appears to have been named after St Helen, mother of Constantine the Great, or Ellen, the Goddess of underground streams, wells and ley lines.

## PART THREE: NEVISON'S BOLT HOLES'

## ACKWORTH OLD HALL

Of course, Nevison had many friends, in many places and was able to come and go in secret at a good number of locations, one of them being the following old hall at Lower Ackworth, being four miles distant from the town of Pontefract situated close to the B6421.

Ackworth Old Hall lays claim to sheltering Nevison from justice, and apparently, this lair was the last known highwayman's hide in the country. The Old Hall, erected in the year 1538 had once been a prestigious farmhouse, having sheltered bailiffs belonging to Nostell Priory. During 1645, one hundred and fifty souls having died from plague and pestilence and in remembrance a plague stone was placed close to the hall. Nevison's hiding place was well hidden being secreted beneath the floor within a bedroom cupboard and the ceiling above the kitchen passageway which was above the bedroom. This passageway ran the whole length of the kitchen ending at the rear exit of the L-shaped Jacobean building. Floorboards were loosened revealing the hidden space where staunch Royalist, Nevison easily concealed himself within the gaping cavity below. Unfortunately, the hide cannot be accessed today since, sadly, the hide was removed to make way for a modern bathroom. It was also common knowledge that an inn at Gleadless, Yorkshire later belonging to Joseph Barker there was a room known as Nevison's Room since the hostelry was often frequented by the highwayman himself.

At the sign of The Black Horse, Bramham Moor, near the crossroads was another of Nevison's haunts this was a most desolate place in its day where coach and horses stopped to rest.

## NEVISON HOUSE

There was another supposed 'safe' house known as Nevison House, where it was stated that Nevison and his beloved bay mare holed up. Nevison House is nestled neatly within the rolling hills close to Thirsk, North Yorkshire (grid ref. 458849). This house is old enough to have sheltered the highwayman and in fact a family of Nevisons', whose names were, William and Stephen, did reside here but not until the 1700's. Interestingly though, on one part of the gable worked in wrought iron were the initials J. and N. Two other bits of wrought iron located on the gable end of the property were curved into the shape of horses' hooves. Local tradition has it that these shoes were from the highwayman's horse which he, Nevison took off and reversed during a snow storm after he had committed another robbery in the district so to confuse the law and believe him to be going away from the scene of the crime! Did this ancient abode really harbour Nevison? Whatever the truth of the matter, there is a secret chamber here hidden deep within the bowels of the cellar. Was Nevison the innovator of shoeing a horse's hoof in reverse in order to confuse the law? Such another happening occurred deep into the night of 11th May 1674 when a gang of nine robbers robbed Hill End Farm near Harden, Bingley tied up the inhabitants to their beds and made away with thousands of pounds worth of gold which they carted to an inn at Collingham where the greedy landlord invented the saying "I want my cut" of the gold, he got what he wanted and was duly hung when the gang were eventually captured!

## ARDSLEY OLD HALL

About three miles east of Barnsley stood Ardsley Old Hall. A moated Manor House set close to Greenside Farm's out buildings before being demolished to make way for the Stairfoot (Stares Foot) roundabout and Ardsley Oaks School car park. They say that Nevison's relative Christopher Nevison lived here and it was commonplace to see the highwayman leading his horse down the street of Ardsley village perhaps coming from the old blacksmith shop on the green.

## PARCEVALL HALL, NEAR SKIPTON

As we know, Nevison had many friends in many places that provided for a consideration, subsistence and shelter for both horse and rider. Close contacts and hiding places were of paramount importance for assured survival, particularly in the case of Nevison, and as we already know, was one of the most daring and dashing thieves in the business. There was not one man in the kingdom that might rival him. Legend has it that he roamed the highways and byways in and around Skipton demanding money from wealthy travellers. When things became too hot for comfort he would simply go to ground in one of his carefully selected retreats.

Parcevall Hall, erected in 1584 (it was once known as Parcevall Farm) nr Skipton and Appletreewick upper Wharfdale, North Yorkshire was one such lair where Nevison sort sanctuary. On admittance he retired to an upstairs chamber where he had superb views over the rolling Yorkshire Dales, having in those days an uninterrupted landscape view in the direction of Skipton, North Yorkshire.

View from the Highwayman's room

The County Sheriff and his constables were known to have come searching for Nevison at the old hall on at least one occasion, but were unsuccessful in catching their quarry. Perhaps it was on one such visit when Nevison fled towards Trollers Gill, Nidderdale...

There are stone steps on the upper floor that eventually lead one to the room Nevison occupied. Today it is still known as The Highwayman's Room. From the chamber window, he had a most excellent view of the surrounding countryside. When he sensed danger approaching he raced into the chamber situated in the next room to his. Here he pressed a secret wooden panel (now blocked up) leading directly to the stable below where his famous bay mare would be ready and waiting to carry her beloved master to safety. Onwards towards Pateley Bridge or Trollers Gill he rode even as the sheriff was banging on the door of Parcevall Hall. The dwelling was once owned by the Yorke family until it was acquired by George Demaine he in turn passed the property to his daughter on her marriage to Christopher Lowson as a wedding gift during the time of Nevison. In the 1960's after the demise of the then owner Sir William Milner bequeathed the building to Our Lady of Walsingham being in the care of Trustees under the title of Walsingham College Yorkshire Properties Limited. Oddly, it is still used as a place of sanctuary being a place of religious retreat.

There is a peculiar story about the hall relating to a certain ghostly figure. It was in the 1960's that a caretaker reported hearing ghostly footsteps issuing from the upper floor of Parcevall Hall. Upon tentative investigation the

Parcevall Hall near Skipton

man swore blind that he witnessed a dark figure suddenly "loom up in front of him." The experience really frightened him. Another spooky happening was when three workmen were working late at the hall one evening. On hearing a noise upstairs coming from the small room nearest the stairs the bravest of them gingerly climbed the staircase armed with a lump hammer in his hand. The next thing he remembers is running back down with the hammer following on behind him! It took ages before the poor fellow calmed down after receiving such a fright. However, a workman staying in Nevison's room for a whole month experienced absolutely nothing. He reported neither seeing nor hearing anything out-of-the-ordinary.

# SWAINBY

Swainby, earlier known as Whorlton, is in the Hambleton District of North Yorkshire. Today's A172 road cuts over the old cattle drovers' road, heading towards a winding hill, known as Worm, or Whorl Hill, passing Blackhorse Farm. This old homestead once served as a wayside inn, and it is to this hostelry, that Nevison was supposed to have called.

## AT THE SIGN OF THE BLACK HORSE

The Black Horse Inn, Bramham, was used by Nevison as a regular rendezvous; he was known to have stabled his mare here when she needed food and rest. The building still exists today but as with many similar alehouses was converted to a farmhouse standing southwards of Bramham crossroads. Bramham is about half way between Leeds and York.

## WENTBRIDGE AND BROCKDALE

The Doncaster to Tadcaster road was deemed a Class II road because; "Although the road has a fine surface throughout it is very hilly. The hills at Wentbridge are dangerous." An ancient stone bridge here carried the wayfarer over the River Went which flows through a really steep valley particularly on the Northern side. This was pure Nevison country. The road today is nought more than a narrow bridle path. The Bluebell Inn has survived, but was in such need of repair, that it was taken down, and rebuilt, using the original materials as much as possible in 1974. Nevison called in here to collect his dues, offering his protection against the onslaught of other knaves and High Toby's such as himself.

Rather than staying at the Bluebell, Nevison preferred to spend his time at the sign of the Old Gate Inn, also situated in the village of Wentbridge. Sadly the Old Gate Inn did not survive. The building was said to have stood close to the corner of a road which points toward The Fox and Hounds and Thorp Audlin.

### 140 DONCASTER TO TADCASTER.

**Description.**—Class II. Although the road has a fine surface throughout, it is very hilly. The hills at Wentbridge are dangerous.

**Gradients.**—At 7m. 1 in 20; 10½m. 1 in 16 (dangerous); 11m. 1 in 14 (dangerous).

**Milestones.**—Measured from Guildhall, Doncaster, as far as Ferrybridge, thereafter from Tadcaster.

**Measurements.**
Doncaster, Town Clock.
10¾  Wentbridge.*
15¼  4½  Ferrybridge.*
27¼  16¾  12¾  Tadcaster.*

**Principal Objects of Interest.**—6½m. Robin Hood's Well. Wentbridge: Smeaton Craggs. Ferrybridge: Fryston Hall, Church. 25m. Towton Battlefield, 1461.

Hotels or Inns at places marked *, and at Bodles Inn, Darrington, and Barkston Ash.

**ROUTE 140. DONCASTER TO TADCASTER.**

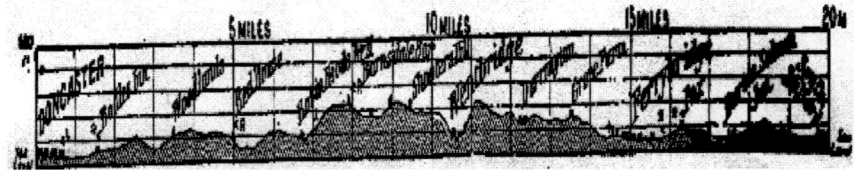

The Contour Road Book 1911

Fletcher's description of one hundred years ago of Wentbridge still stands today as it did even in Nevison's day. He writes; "Few villages in Yorkshire are so picturesquely situated as Wentbridge. From its southern point on the Great North Road-redolent with memories of the good old days when highwaymen and post-chaises, run away lovers and mail coaches were as thick as blackberries-drop suddenly down through the woods.... past the famous Bluebell Inn to the bridge spanning the Went, only to rise again on the shoulder of Went Hill on the other side, to the undulating land stretching towards Ferrybridge. Looking eastward from the bridge the Wend winds in delightful curves along an ever- narrowing valley until it is lost to sight amidst the woods of Brockdale... " A place where witches and beggars" lived. Mary Pannell, the famous Yorkshire witch, once dwelled in a limestone cave here, overlooking the River Went. She was put to death in the early 17th century.

Darrington is the next village to Wentbridge where the Old North Road crossed the Pontefract-Wormersly road.

### CAPTAIN NEVISON, A CRAVEN LEGEND.

Who has not seen one of those evenings — when the sun is characteristically said to be set in blood; when all the western sky is filled with a red and lurid glare, relieved only by the dark masses of rolling clouds; when all the ait is gloomy still, and a sense of oppression seems to hang on living and inanimate things. It was on such an evening that a spectator on Brunton Heights might have seen the brown wastes of Burn Moor, stretching away to the horizon, and reaching the thickly wooded plain beneath him, not studded as now with the quite homestead, or the highly cultivated tract, but one long, cheerless solitude. He might have seen, too, the whole extent of the deep and melancholy forests of Lawkland, the tops of whose lurid pines contrasted well with the gloomy sunset.

Barely might he have decried a single horseman dashing wildly along from the moor towards the forest, and had he been nearer he would have detected the horse's jaded gallop, and the rider's repeated and hurried glance behind him. The stalwart figure, erect bearing, the holster's pistols and cutlasses, gave a military appearance to the rider, but his dress stamped him rather as one of those daring and desperate marauders whose deeds at that time inspired terror in the unprotected home and unguarded traveller.

He wore high jack boots, armed with a formidable rowel, and (pointed part of a spur which turns on an axis). A long lapelled and closely fitting coat of archer's green, embroidered vest, and a slouch hat. His features, though stamped with the impress of fierce passions, and haggard with anxiety, were peculiarly handsome, and his sinewy frame seemed filled for deeds of hardihood and daring. Widely was Captain Nevison (for such was the name he bore) known by sight, but still more widely known by fame.

Strange may it seem to us in this our day, that a marauder like Nevison, whose crime it 'twere difficult to recount, could brazen the light of noonday among those who knew him well; but the lamentable state of the law at that time as regards detection and apprehension fully accounts for the bold front which the highwayman put on.

Nevison had committed a highway robbery in the neighbourhood of Ambleside, (Cumbria) attended with circumstances of peculiar atrocity, and almost immediately afterwards was heard of joining in a boisterous revel at a remote hostelry, at no great distance from the scene of the deed. The officers of the law, accompanied with several well mounted gentlemen, at length resolved to capture... Nevison, on receiving warning of the fact, had time to throw himself on the valuable horse that had long borne him through every danger, before his pursuers came into sight. A long unremitting gallop considerably lengthened the distance between the robber and his pursuers; yet still, by means of a relay of horses, they sometimes caught a view of him as he dashed over the top of some hill. For miles his horse held gallantly on, and ford and banks and waste swept quickly past him. Burn Moor was reached, and here he became sensible that his horse's strength was failing; still he spared not the spur, though the ground that endurance, and as he reached the narrow bridle-path that wound through the forest of Lawkland it was plain that if urged much further this would be its last gallop. One keen and hurried glance the robber cast behind him as he entered the forest depths and saw to his dismay the nearer approach of his pursuers as they merged into sight over Burn Moor.

On! On! Still with a last panting strain the gallant beast answered to the spur, and, broke madly on. A murky twilight drew on apace, and deeper grew the forest; the steed's long gallop broke rudely on the stillness, and the pheasant sprang scared away; the dismal echoes sounded harshly in the robber's ears, and bold as he was he reluctantly felt the gloomy influence of a place like this.

Still on! The wild ravine was neared: the pine trees are taller and gloomier and closer there, and no bubbling stream runs down the rocky ground, but the enchanter's nightshade and the henbane flourish among the huge tumbled moss-grown stones.

One broad chasm must be leapt, and the forest path grows wilder and more passable; a bound and the robber gained the open-space, but it was his horse's last effort, and he sank with his rider exhausted to the ground.

"S' blood," muttered Nevison, as he recovered his feet, "the game is up, and yet I know these haunts well, and they may hide me from these bloodhounds yet." As he spoke an enchantingly sweet voice broke on his ear thus: -

> Horseman! ride!
> The angry tide
> Of hot pursuit is on thee;
> The hounds of prey
> Are on their way,
> And death has well nigh won thee."

The robber turned, a graceful female figure sat at the foot of a stunted fir; coal black hair floated around features of a deathly paleness but wondrous beauty, and an unearthly light streamed from her dark eyes. "Soho! My pretty one," exclaimed Nevison. "Thou lovest mockery; aye! Thou hast a daring eye, and what a fitting mate for a daring; I will e'en tarry here to woo thee." "Soho! My pretty one," exclaimed Nevison. "Thou lovest mockery; aye! Thou hast a daring eye, and what a fitting mate for a daring; I will e'en tarry here to woo thee."

With taper in hand pointing across the chasm, and a smile of scorn curling her lip, she said —

"Freebooter, I love thy light tone of boldness, but thou mightiest rue the wooing of such as me. I tell thee, thy delay is death, - aha! Death, - 'tis a merry word; but listen, down, down in the depths of yon chasm in a dark cavern hangs an enchanted bridle, within a magic circle that none but the bold may touch. Art thou bold?""I love not this devilry." Replied the robber, "but my heart quails not." "Tis well; the horse that bears this bridle will never flag, but will bear thee fleeting as an arrow, and untiring as the sun. Wilt thou win it?"
"Tis a bargain, most dainty fiend; yet show me how."
"The bridle touched by this wand shall be safely thine."
The robber grasped it with well-nerved hand.
"Yet, one warning" the lady goblin said, "No other influence but that of those enchanted reins must urge thy steed along; no spur or human voice must mix with the spirit of enchantment. If thou heedest not this warning, a weary doom is thine, an ever jaded gallop, and an agonizing dread of pursuit."

Ere the robber could reply, her figure vanished with an eldritch laugh. He lingered not long in doubt, but strode with heavy steps towards the chasm, muttering as he went. "I care not, I'll find this wondrous bridle if the devil is in it, as doubtless he is. Aye! 'twould be a glorious rid, and her demon warning bootless." Down one side of the chasm the freebooter with difficulty descended, clinging to many a jutting stone and stunted bush. He reached the bottom, and as he groped blindly on he felt the damp and chill air of a cavern surround him; still he held on amid palpable darkness; at length a phosphorescent light broke upon his sight.
"Tis here; the witch spoke the truth."

A few steps brought him to the wall of the cavern, and within a magic circle hung a heavily bitted and ornamented bridle.

"Now brave heart," the robber cried, and one touch of the wand he bore brought the bridle from within the magic circle to the ground. He grasped it, and, as fast as the darkness would permit retraced his steps. He reached the edge of the cavern in safety. The steed still lay panting and exhausted on the long tangled and dark grass. A moment sufficed to throw the enchanted reins over its head, and it sprang with a bound to its feet — the robber vaulted into the saddle, and away they cleft the air like a wild and rushing wind.

It seemed but a brief few moments ere they reached the foot of Giggleswick Scar, but the steed paused not there; with snorting breath and fiery speed it dashed up an opening in the cliff (still known today as Nevison's Leap), and away over broken rock and sunken ground, across field and flood, and hill and waste. Wildly he swept past the mountain tarn of Malham, as it lay coldly and darkly still in the pale dull tarn of Malham, as it lay coldly and darkly still in the pale dull moonlight. Away! Over rocks again; and now the chasm of Gordale draws near, where the tumbling waters are boiling fathoms deep below. "On my brave steed," the robber cried in wild glee at his hurricane speed, and buried the rowel in the horse's side as it leapt the fearful gulf. The spell was broken, the enchanted bridle gone — gone to its old resting place, the magic circle in the cold cavern at Lawkland. The rushing joy of the robber's blood ebbed away. Dread again seized his heart, and he turned shuddering as if to look for his pursuers — and still, but with jaded gallop, the steed went on.

The lonely midnight traveller on Malham Moor (if such there be) will yet at times hear the sound of a viewless horseman borne on the wind — 'tis Nevison on his matchless aimless gallop — ever flying from an imaginary pursuit — his horse all panting and exhausted, yet still pressing away.

A cleft in the steep face of Giggleswick Scar is still known as the place where it was that Nevison's steed climbed the Scar. The Ordnance Map names this as "Nevison's Nick." Whilst perusing old archives housed on dusty shelves in a darkened corner of Keighley Library my eye fell upon a tome containing the above story of Mr John Nevison, Gentleman Highwayman of the North. The original story comes from the pages of No. 1 of the Giggleswick Grammar School Olio, published in the year 1845.

Note; There is no exact evidence that Nevison actually visited Ambleside there is a William Nevison listed in records held by the Cumbrian Record Office covering 16th-20th century donated by the Browne family of Towne End, Troutbeck, Westmoreland which says that one William Nevison is listed in the Heraldic Seal of 1792-1 79. Since the Nevisons are said to have roots in Cumberland it is tempting to believe that the highwayman may have been visiting relatives at the time of the supposed robbery.

## THE EBBING AND FLOWING WELL, GIGGLESWICK

There is yet another local legend of the magic bridle and the "spirit of the well" connected to Nevison published by William Smith 1890. The author describes a "a curious old picture (engraved by Buck and Feary dated 1778) from this it seems that the well was at that day situated a short distance above the road (the new highway runs higher up and close to the well), and from it two copious streams flowed into Giggleswick Tarn, which then lay at the foot of the scar; the road crossing the head of the tarn by a ford. The inscription at the foot of the engraving is as follows:

"The amazing Flowing and Ebbing Well in Giggleswick Scarr, in the road to Kendal. "...When the water in the well is at its lowest point, there may be occasionally be seen what is known as the silver thread."

This is nothing more than a tiny current of air running from end to end of the well, but on account of it's rare appearance the superstitious consider it as a token of good luck to the person who is privilaged to see it. It was the "spirit of the well" that, according to the local legend, gave the magic bridle to Nevison, the highwayman, when he was pursued, by the aid of which he was able to ride up Giggleswick Scars at the point still known as "Nevison's Nick," where upon he leaped over the chasm at the head of Gordale. Many writers, including Mr. Barnaby, and others, have all made mention of this curious well.

The Ebbing and Flowing well
Gigglewick

## POLYOLBION (in part)

'At Giggleswick, where I a fountain can you show

That eight times a day is said to ebb and flow

Who sometime was a nymph, and mountains high

Of Craven, whose blue heads for caps put on sky.

Amongst the Oreads there, and Sylvans made abode

(It was ere human foot upon these hills had trod)

Of all the mountain kind, and, since she was most fair

It was a Satyr's chance to see her silver hair

Flow loosely at her back, as up a cliffe she clame,

Her beauties noting well her features, and her frame.

And after her he goes; when which she did espy

Before him like the wind the nimble nymph doth fly;

## CHURCH OF St. ALKELDA, GIGGLESWICK

Only one of two churches in the land bear the name of Alkelda. The Giggleswick church dates from the 15th century, and, in Nevison's day, was used to house Cromwell's troops. A stained glass window within the church depicts its patron saint, a supposed Saxon lady of great standing who, legend has it, was strangled to death by two Pagan Danish woman for refusing to give up her faith on 28th day of March 800 A.D. (Richard II gave his permission for a fair to be held on this day in honour of this saint in 1388).

A stone tomb was unearthed during excavations at nearby Middleham Church also known as St. Alkelda containing ancient remains of a female. Was this then, the body of the mysterious lady, St. Alkelda? Nobody really knows for certain whether Alkelda existed for there is almost nothing in the annals to confirm her earthly presence. Michael Slater believes that Alkelda's name may have actually been Alchhild — Saxon meaning high born. She was supposed to have been murdered in a field close to the Middleham church, yet it is a stained glass window in St. Alkelda's Church, Giggleswick which depicts the crime. Incidently, there is a similar story concerning St. Mary the Virgin, in Leake near Nevison House near Thirsk which speaks of when the woman of Leake rose up as one to fight Danish invaders. The women slew all the Pagans who dared enter into their village.

St. Alkelda is invoked against eye troubles, and she is also the patron saint of the curious Ebbing and Flowing well. The window in St. Alkeldas' Church shows that there may

Church of St. Akelda

have been certain sacrifices practiced at this 'holy well'. Perhaps then, the 'spirit' legend may have been drawn from the story of St. Alkelda. Did Michael Drayton base his poem on the sainted Alkelda written long before Nevison's fated meeting with the 'spirit' of the well? Another interesting fact worth mentioning is that Sir Richard Tempest Knight (c1425 -1488) was interred in a vault within the Giggleswick church in 1488. He is buried beneath the floor of the Tempest Chantry alongside the head of his best war-horse!

His effigy is located nearby. Tempest was knighted at the Battle of Wakefield by Lord Clifford in 1460 and fought in the Wars of the Roses on the Lancaster side. In 1461 he was accused of treason but was forgiven by Edward IV.

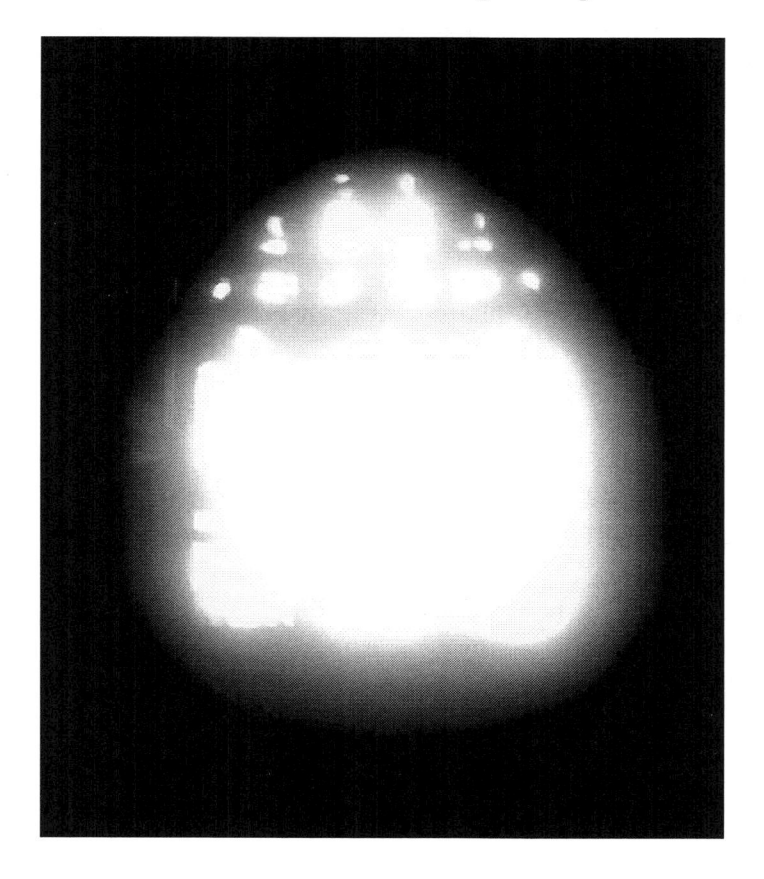

Inside the old church looking northwards towards the stained glass window depicting the ebbing and flowing well.

## PONTEFRACT'S NEVISON'S LEAP

According to history our knight-of-the-road had many a breathtaking escape from the law. Nevison's cunning, as previously noted kept him well-ahead of the pack. His bravery and his horsemanship were second to none. Nevison was fearless on the road in his quest for money and adventure as we have already witnessed from his many daring escapades.

Nevison and his faithful mare were witnessed to have made not one (as in the case of the Ebbing and Flowing Well)) but two hair rising leaps in order to evade arrest. His second amazing jump over a narrow gorge (a deep cut between rocks) happened between Ferrybridge and Pontefract, South Yorkshire. The village and an inn close by still bears his name even today it is known as Nevison's Leap Hotel — a testament of his fantastic feat. Ferrybridge being the crossing point of the River Aire. This area was also a most a popular coaching destination being situated on the Old North Road, deeply rutted when muddy but having easy access to both the North and South of England. Private horse-drawn coaches belonging to well-heeled society of the day stopped off at this coaching inn also. This particular point must have seemed like easy pickings to both highwaymen and footpads alike. Opportunists of the lowest kind laid wait, quietly lurking in some dark and shadowy place, ready to steal anything from anyone they could from the occupants within such coaches.

Here is another story of Nevison's Leap at Pontefract; Fleeing for his life yet again the highwayman and his mare successfully negotiated a most dangerous wide chasm now known as 'Nevison's Leap' in order to shake off his pursuers who had got too close for comfort. The following story of the "lep" is quoted from Fox's History of Pontefract;

"On the road near St. Thomas' Hill is a deep ravine, cut through the solid rock, forming part of the road, which acquired the name of 'Nevison's Leap' from the following singular tale. Nevison a noted highwayman, having committed a robbery in the neighbourhood of Pontefract, and being closely pressed by his pursuers, in order to make his escape desperately leapt across the road, where the rock is cut through at the greatest width, and thus eluded for a while the grasp of his pursuers." It was a most daring deed and those following were left behind and Nevison once again evaded capture and remained free.

### A NAME TO CONJURE WITH

John Nevison, William Nevison, Swift Nicks, or Johnson? What was his true identity? Some say that it was not Nevison at all who did the York ride but a more mysterious shadowy figure, whose true identity was never revealed, and even his name on two Royal pardon's dated 1667 and 1670 only appeared as 'Swift Nix, gent. Supposed.'

Apparently, this Swift Nix got a Captain's Commission in Ireland sometime in the year of 1674. Nix suffered death by violence in the year 1687.

## NEVISON COAT-OF-ARMS

The family crest is Argent, a chevron, charged with a mullet, between two eaglets displayed, Azure. The Crest, a leopard passant, collared Or, the tail sable. Taken from Dugdale's Visitation 1664.

**Nevison is branch of the clan Campbell.**

The name of Nevison's faithful horse was never recorded. What became of the horse after the arrest of Nevison?